Metamorphosis
Collected poems

Gillian Petrie

Metamorphosis – Collected Poems

Published by Palewell Press Ltd http://www.palewellpress.co.uk/

First Edition

ISBN 978-1-911587-01-9

A CIP catalogue record for this title is available from the British Library.

Palewell Press Ltd supports the Forest Stewardship Council® (FSC®) the leading international forest-certification organisation. Our books carrying the FSC® label are printed on FSC®-certified paper. Their printing and binding complies with ISO 14001 (Environmental Management) and 50001 (Energy Management).

DEDICATION

For Muir Hunter, beloved husband and fellow-poet.

ACKNOWLEDGEMENTS

Versions of some of the poems in this collection have previously appeared in anthologies: *Bedford Square 2,* edited by Sir Andrew Motion (John Murray, 2007), *A Luminous Man – Muir Hunter recalled with love* (Palewell Press, 2013) and in issues of *Starters,* the publications of Kick Start Poets of Salisbury, from 1998 onwards.

CONTENTS

CHILDHOOD

"I have had playmates, I have had companions
In my days of childhood, in my joyful school-days,
All, all are gone, the old familiar faces"
Charles Lamb: The Old Familiar Faces.

Between the Walls

Between the eastern and the western walls
a great parterre was laid,
a quilt of scented roses, gold and pink:
Hebe's Lip, Celestial, Peace;
and in the catmint border, ginger Tom
would sensuously roll,
his tummy to the sun.

I took refuge in an apple-tree:
yearned across the eastern wall
into the flowerless place beyond —
where blesséd loons in their unreason
shuffled down the asphalt paths,

worked as ploughmen, joiners, weavers,
fashioned things in wood and cloth,
broke the chalk to make the graves
that buried them.

I wept for them. My mother said:
Wednesday's child is full of woe,

*   *

Of the people living on the western side,
there's nothing I can usefully say.
I never spoke their language, wore their habits —
learned, instead, from those on the eastern side
how to submit and how to grieve.
I watched them from my tree:

I know.

These days, I accept my station
in the pretty place between.
There are good times in the garden
when the roses open to receive the sun
and I'm reminded of lascivious old Tom.

Only in uncertain darkness do the flints appear,
the arrowheads too sharp for me to bear,
too keen for Sisyphean souls
who happen to be born on Friday:
we whose fate it is to love, to give,
to mourn.

Grave Matters

The place would haunt me less,
or so I thought,
if every night before I slept,
I summoned it to mind:
nailed the image of the shaven grass,
the rows of slabs in tidy lines,
each a lid upon a life.

Those who lay there —
lie there still, for all I know —
were, in that more brutal age,
called 'loonies'. As a child,
I saw the persevering gait,
heard the regal certainty:
I am Queen Victoria.

For the regal one,
and others in her state of grace,
there was no dithering: no
lure of resurrection,
joyous graveyard turf-erupting,
lolling on the gravestones
naked as you please,
awaiting *whoosh*; no
pain in nothingness.

Early Learning

He sat with me at twin desks in the infant class
at Wendy House, his face so close,
a wrinkled boy not fully straightened out —

frowning, as he did my sums for me,
who never could recall the number falling down
below the border into no-man's land;

but perfectly remember his perplexity
as I chopped up his syllables, spoon-fed ten-
der mouthfuls he could never learn to chew.

Cross-breeding pair, we perched on our perfidious wire —
then, wordlessly, he flew away, leaving me to steer
without my navigating star.

Munich, 1938

Blood-red poppies blaze in their herbaceous bed.
Voices dribble through the open window.
From the hammock strung between
the monkey-puzzle trees,
I listen to the mutterings about the Somme,
slaughter that was summer-long —

and there is Raymond, soldier in a silver frame, among
her Coty creams and dressing-table things.

Mother plays her sad song on the gramophone:
when I grow too old to dream....

I take a snapshot of the garden with my new
Box Brownie:
place the poppies centre-frame,
colour bleeding into black-and-white:
Raymond's face before the final battle.

Father says: *the line can't hold.*

Peace, insist the fruity voices on the News,
In Our Time.

Apple Tree, 1939-40

I bike to school along the coastal plain,
beside the empty beach.
Antoinette, who lives inland,
comes by double-decker honey-bus.
We meet, as usual, in the branches of the apple
tree: listen to the gunfire from the Channel.
A*s the crow flies only twenty miles across,*
but all they talk about in class
are *highland clearances.*
Do they mean the southern downs,
those naked giants lying half-way up the sky,
those treeless hills that Antoinette rides
on her way to school?   Is a *clearance*
just a word for *making ready*
as the autumn fog of thirty-nine
deletes the line between our childhood
and the dread. Sound is muffled,
mothers bend their heads to sew
the black-out. We collect the windfalls,
eat the better bits.

One day, honey-bus arrives:
there's no Antoinette. Where is she?
No-one seems to know.
I ask my father to explain the clearances.
Perhaps she has been *cleared.*
But he says, only:
that is why you're English, as we listen
to the bombers nosing through the fog,
checking out the coastline, heading
for the places where the apple-trees
no longer grow.

Going to church, 1940-41

We climbed the street to church,
bitter winter, forty-one,
looking out towards the Lizard Head,
the submarines like killer sharks
intent on feeding at our shores.

The Gothic church, in Lenten mourning,
draped the virgin in a purple shroud.
The priest wore purple,
hands and feet were purple;
granite pillars dripped
and incense hung like clouds of breath.

Our cloaks were dark and thick
and we would shrink within our witches' hoods:
frozen song-birds
mutely huddled in the pews.

Ides of March, thaw began
and snowdrops drowned.
I took to my bed with a fever:
hummed,
softly at first,
under the covers.

Then took a deep breath and began to sing.

Doodlebug Games, 1944

Night of war — another night of bedding
in a corridor —
counting down the missiles as they grumble overhead —
the engine cuts
a beat before the thing explodes — that will-it-won't-it moment
as it falls —
this time on the chapel — smashing through the roof —
blasting out
bejewelled saints in ruby robes — glassy lifeblood
raining down —
come the morning — climb the stairs — five-inch bath —
tepid puddle —
teacher says go out and read — gather up
our history books —
Tudors to the Act of eighteen-thirty-two — funny cut-
off point —
rather like the stop-dead-mid-air doodlebugs
before they drop —
use the books as cricket bats — ball as hard as iron — worse
than any doodlebug —
Lizzie Lightfoot laid out cold — lying in a heap of Tudors —
teacher-ticking-off
suspended — saved again by screaming siren —
Lizzie never quite the same.

ARS POETICA

"Poesy was ever thought to have some participation
of divineness..."
Francis Bacon (1561-1626): Advancement of Learning

Into Being

Your poems are born between sleeping and waking,
are borne through the space between pain and relief.
between the eyelid and the cheek—

they are crying out to happen; they will catch your breath
that they may live to celebrate
this green May morning;

knowing that no other being, save yourself,
can shape them, use the stamp of love, sing that
peculiar lullaby.

Plain Chant

Know your place
with Calliope.   She will brew the vat
the way   she's minded to
however long   it takes; so
limber up   with crosswords, sad words,
keep her clicking   through synapses
synonyms   and parts of speech
even as   she's swimming in your
bloodstream   looking for
exactitude.

Disallow
approximation,   Latin-based
embellishment,   words dressed up in overkill
for purposes   of excitation.
Go for   scullion-speech
the lingo   of the peasantry,
the catch-phrase   of the street:
you cannot test   integrity
until you bite   the pearl and leave
no scar.

And even now —
when you begin   to string your lyric
in your sad   suburban room
though gladdened   by the daffodils
whose heads   will nod when they have drunk
their fill —   beware a note that's flat,
a syllable   whose stress
is not   how you would want it heard,
a word   that fails
to ring.

Sleight of Hand: for Elizabeth Bishop, poet and painter

No desire to overplay a hand too slight
to span an octave: not
so much an iron hand in velvet glove,
more a seedling
clenched within a husk.

To paint, use either hand.
For vertices, the canopies of trees,
hairs and fronds and blades of grass,
dexter, steady keeper of the brush;
sinister,
the stubby finger for the smudging of horizons,
highfalutin clouds;

balance left and right,
drawing lines with certainty between
the shadow and the light.

Dying apples on the canvas,
comice pears with ageing skins,
drown beneath a fiercely blue tsunami —
not the background she envisaged,
not the upshot.
Not art, not at all —.
for all its vicious beauty
nothing but a trick.

Crossed Out

> *"I have crossed out all I wrote last night & more, cursed & bored and raging": Philip Larkin to Monica Jones, 23 May 1962.*

Muse,
just tell me your intention.
I will follow where you lead,
but what's our destination?
Do my absences annoy you?
Do you sulk when I allow
the current thing to lurk in shadow,
grow a tightly-knitted lichen jacket
as I dream or check the Footsie,
hoping that arrangements will be put in place
behind my back?

Take the latest poem — yes, do take it;
it's completely out of hand —
I inferred that we were working on a theme
of black and white,
good or evil, what you will,
point and counterpoint, perhaps.
I followed meekly down your path,
wrote of my engraving:
people grouped beside the Thames
at Twickenham —
eighteen sixteen, achromatic,
foxed by time and too much light.

But then, without consulting me,
you pulled Jane Austen in because, presumably,
you spotted Emma in her cape and bonnet
bossing all the picnickers about:
saw in that stove-hatted figure stiffly standing
Mister Knightley, disapproving.
Hardly black and white.
Of all the courtships in the canon,
it's the least conventional.

In your defence, no doubt, you'll say
you gave me that most precious gene,
the gift of verbal echoing. I thank you
but I wish you'd leave my plots alone.
What makes you think that it was Emma by the river?
She preferred Box Hill, of course.
No wonder Larkin got so cross.

HOOPS OF STEEL

"Those friends thou hast and their adoption tried
Grapple them to thy soul with hoops of steel"
William Shakespeare: Hamlet

Icon

Beloved daughter,
as you leave to cross the seas and plains,
you'll find a present
wrapped between the layers
of your trousseau:

an apportionment of streaky onyx,
creamy-green,
crafted as a woman-head,
Kisii daughter of a chieftain,
striæ channelling her cheeks
as tears that dry
uncomforted.

Despite her grief —
she, too, has travelled far —
she will survive, this warrior-
woman:
tussle where she must,
tilting raked and braided hair
akin to winter-seeded rows of manioc —

/continued

ever mindful of their prickly shoots
on bare-foot journeys
through the *bundu,* (*)
balancing the water-cruse so that no drop is spilled.

London child,
do not pine for your beloved, dirty city.
Keep the icon near your hearth, wherever that may be.
Lay your own head
on a soon-to-be-familiar pillow.
Be at ease

* *Tribal territory*

First-born

The summer solstice night —
never wholly dark—
was slow to yield you up.

The midnight sun, a cryptic presence,
fell upon my struggle
to give you life.

It crossed my mind that we might stay
forever tied
but you found your way

into the light of a glorious morning.
Calm and curious
wearing a little frown

you came at noon, on a wave of relief
to the sound
of exuberant bells.

How like a winter has your absence been...

...what dark days seen.
Even though my other life was full of happiness,
your absence was a stain of deep despair.
I could not know that you would ever reappear,
forgive whatever there was to forgive,
call me Muv.

I learned much later that you used the time
to study, use your subtle mind, your perfect pitch,
initiative,

Then, one evening, as I finished washing-up,
the phone rang, That brief conversation
(about words, what else?) restored our unpossessed
integrity.

Title is a quotation from Sonnet 97, William Shakespeare

Another Victoria: for Victoria Vallance, 1870-1938

Take my seed, my little seedlings, and assume
your forebear's genes: the beauty and the courage
of Victoria,
whose image, creamy skin and auburn hair,
hangs today serenely on my wall;

who sailed way back then
with her Albert to Ceylon,
bought from merchants for a pittance
rough, unpolished gemstones you could toss about
to catch the sun,
who would delight in formal visits
from the jungle elephants to introduce their young;
endured the death of her beloved Albert;
brought her jewels home;

raised her daughters and her son
to speak the truth and shame the devil,
as the saying goes;

and I remember

walking with her in the gardens in the summertime,
talking of *her* granny's service to the Queen;
going to the Silver Jubilee,
the rain which soaked her crimson hat
and turned her hair a shocking pink —
and how we laughed

/continued

and how we laughed
until she died, far too young, at sixty-eight
when I was eight:
lying as she does today against a churchyard wall,
the stone incised *Her children Call Her Blesséd.*

For my part, I wear her golden chain
in perpetuity.

In Tranquillity: for my daughter, Sarah

She is home — whose life was threatened.
She is, for the moment, safe.
We can meet; meander through the country shop,
assess the jerseys, gilets, fleeces.
Though she's always silent,
it's apparent what she likes:

dismissive wave at garments that are coarse or nubbly,
fingering, instead,
the silk or soft or sensuous,
inhaling after-shopping cups of latte
(baby at adjoining table shrieking)
sweet normality of things.

In a while, when I'm more peaceful,
I will find the metaphor, the proper shape or form —
Dantesque, heroic, dithyrambic, anapaestic —
sprinkled with alliteration: tell you
of my tension in poetic rhythm
when she nearly died.
For the moment
humdrum's good enough.

Bequest to Sarah

Beloved, I leave you this painting,
the small one near my bed.

They will explain it is for you;
when you see it, you will know it,

stretch your green eyes as you do,
although you seldom speak

except to say my name. Take it
please: this map, this future land

where you and I can talk together
by the trees, beside the lake,

where pale water funnels into pale sky:
and there's no horizon.

Painting the Sea

I keep your presents in a little chest,
a curl of bladder-wrack in mourning for the sea,
a silver abalone shell,
your naive watercolours:
tugs and trawlers,
skiffs and schooners,
washed in child-paintbox-green.

Even as you die
you move your hand across the sheet
as if to trim a sail in the wind
or paint a scene.

I take the hand:
I love you.

Astonished eyes, blazing blue,
register the lie —
never love on either part,
only a pity most profound.

I watch you
going aground.

You know the difference —
so do I.

Second Skin

Towards the end,
she would not change the dress
except to sleep:
stretchy woolly, cocoa brown,
familiar in its spills and relics,
holes and tears,
comfort-smell —

saw me looking:
it won't wash, she said —

I knew her former self would be appalled;
I listened to that voice and as she slept
I stole the dress,
stitched it, washed it,
hung it up to dry at dawn.

She went up close
and then pulled back
as though confronted by an alien thing:
it had ceased to be her skin.

Eye

I burnish up the tiger's eye,
only gem you ever gave me,
dark disturbance swimming in the iris;
hang it on a silver chain,
clingstone in the hollow
of my collar-bone.

Cannot meet your inattentive eye
nor yet the half-smile in your glance:
they speak too much of your ambivalence.
Keep the photo in my bag,
drum the cardboard
with my fingers;

drive towards the estuary, a space
we'd travelled many times,
along the iron, dactylic bridge,
above the tidal waters of the spring,
running hard against the current,
quarrelling;

on this, at least, we were agreed,
it was the place:
so far to fall,
so deep the river as it meets the sea,
so burdensome the eye.

Grief in Wlodawa

Ravens agitate the poplar trees
marching through the Pomeranian plain,
the conquerors' corridor;

a river bank, a
grassy bridge, bisected by a single wire,
mark the border.

On the western side,
furrows turned by horse-drawn plough
rule the earth.

Beyond the wire,
mist obscures the empty marsh,
bird-less sky.

The light fades
in the hospice chapel
as the child dies.

Grandmothers —
she and I —
weep.

Dreaming of Light: according to Sarah

the house
is different from the other place
called house

the bed is soft
it has a mother-smell
I sleep

the light is all around
sounding
like the light

that licks
the bluish water into white
sips

the salt
blowing past the face
and hair

sings
of sun and sea and sky
and air

*   *

the song
when I awake is gone
my words are lost
I cannot taste the music
or the colour
of the light

it’s not a sighing
or a singing
light

Singer in the Dusk: Homage to Gluck

Che faro senza Euridice
fills the room.
She hisses, sotto voce:
turn that music off.
He knows the score, thought it fitting
for his own farewell;
tired, drops his hand.

Notes are not allowed.
Minutes must be measured
by the stitches in her quilt.
She has reached the border.
It is time.

He repents their days and nights,
thinks with longing of the other one,
the primavera of the tumbling hair
and tender hands,
the lyre-caressing
singer
in the dusk.

No matter, for the aria flows
note-perfect through his head.
He summons up his repertoire,
sweet-and-slow
oboe d'amore,
trumpets blowing on the spark
until the moment when the quilt is spread —
Piu dolce libertá.

CRY HAVOC

"Cry havoc and let slip the dogs of war."
William Shakespeare: Julius Caesar

No Ceasefire

Sunrise promised heat and happiness,
a truce.

Talks on the hill, above the mist,
continued into the dusk.

There should have been a ceasefire.
We should have been able to head

for the square,
dance the midsummer night away,

fall asleep, as dawn broke,
together.

But the guns began again.
You were running across the open space,

the no-man's land,
to meet me.

Clan Warfare

His clan had marched up from the borders
through the Strath of Orchy, mine had crossed
the Fault by Keppanach. He wanted passage
to the west: I, over-wintering for the kine.

We clashed between the Corries
where the treacle-burn meanders through the glen,
and lings as tough as whips for penance
may not be uprooted by the hand.

We looked into a well where no light shone —
each dropped a stone. Their chief is tall:
distaff hair, translucid eyes, unreadable.
We talked of coveted terrain.

Our restless men about us stamped their feet,
drew their claymores, slammed them back.
I knew the other clan for traitorous folk,
but hands were shaken on a kind of pact.

My clansmen settled in the glen around a fire
and sang their island airs. I had not reckoned on
the thick mist closing in, the swoop at midnight
from the hills, slaughter of my kin.

Left for dead, I sailed the oceans, swore allegiance
to an English king. But my descendents
bear the name: like the tightly-threaded ling
may never be uprooted from their land.

Intaglio

> *The bust of a Sumerian woman, BC 3000, was stolen, in 2003, from a Baghdad museum.*

The bomb falls on Baghdad:
the building crumbles
into rubble-dust.
I stumble on what looks
to be a severed head, one
not made of flesh and bone;
blow the dust away,
stroke the coiled hair
dabbed on by the sculptor's
spatula;
                        the slash
which now encircles
the Sumerian brow
which then have borne a fillet
of intaglio,
oyster pearls
embedded in the gold,
empty sockets
filled with irises
of lapis lazuli,

/continued

Her cheekbones,
miracles of chiselling,
are barely dented by the fall;
her lips are stopped upon a breath.
I dig a grave of clay
outside the city walls,
a swallow-hole
to nest the looping hair,
a measured hollow
for the limbs
that never were.

Gdańsk, 1989

Early light:
people walking, eyes down, on the street
of April Twenty-Fifth: sniffing out the morning bread,
threading string through rolls of paper,
garlanding.

Black swans
skim the shallows of the Baltic;
on the top of long-cooled chimneys,
storks look down from neatly-
woven nests.

Solidarity erupts;
shipyard workers raise their giant crosses;
scrawl their slogan, *Solidarnosc,*
light a thousand candles up and down
the plain;

people learn
to meet the eyes of others on the street,
recall the text:
to everything a season
and a time.

Kiev, 1989, 2004, 2013

In the square of Independence
early winter hail
wetly falls on woollen hats and pale faces:

some who'd raised their fists and giant crosses
years before
in the name of *Solidarnosc* —

fought and won the Orange Revolution,
built the shrines to martyred priests and radicals
whose souls flame on

in candles lit across the central plain,
the corridor which stretches from the Baltic
through Ukraine: now

the thousands in the square of Independence know
it's time to come together
yet again.

Cult

I have been chosen —
one of the few
willing and ready
to hear the Truth.

Stay with us. Sever ties
with those
who seek
to undermine.

I leave my other life behind.

Facts are not Truth.
Truth is Faith.
Faith will come
if you work and pray.

I bend my head,

dig the rubble
as the sun goes down
shovel gold
into their hands:

keep shovelling.

Your reward will be
in Heaven,
they say,

knowing me to be
the fool I am.

Demurrer: for David Kelly, 1944-2003

Shame stalked with him as he climbed to Harrowdown,
treading bracken,
early afternoon.

Never met such plunderers before — they broke his own belief,
snapped his spirit
like a twig,

Nonetheless, it moves.

It's calm up here at Harrowdown, the air is still.
In their house, below, she is asleep.
Thank God, she is asleep.

Here, Iraq, your weapons of destruction: pills, a noose,
a kitchen knife.
No threat.

Dog Days, 2004: for Kenneth Bigley

Dog-stars dog the cosmos:
Procyon brings close air,
hot rain,
leaf-curl,
lies,
conspiracies and worse.

Mid-August, nights draw in —
late September
guelder roses shed their leaves,
flower nakedly on thorns;
dawns come darkly in
with silent rain.

Images of flood:
water thick as treacle
vomits
ten-ton lorries, pairs of houses
into the Atlantic.
Many weep for loss
of bedding lovers, lover-beds.

No beds for those who huddle
in the desert,
flimsy-veiled against the wind
and dust —
insects feeding on organic matter,
excrement and weeping
eyes.

/continued

Elsewhere, bane
of Sirius,
whose satellites beam footage
of an eastern massacre:
grubby, naked children, grey as death
scampering for their lives
through potholed streets —

the sound track is a keening on a single note,
the universal sound of grieving
for the dead,
for the nearly dead grey engineer
caged and shackled
with a look
none should ever have to wear
and no-one see.

Up in Flames

It happened, so they tell me,
in the middle of the night:
my canvas faces
shrivelled to a heap of body powder,
panes of shattered glass through which my sketches,
mutilated fantasies,
took flight.

I mourn them,
those forever-lost experiments,
many executed in the early hours
when consciousness
collides with dreaming.

I take comfort from the finished works
which hang in galleries and in the halls
of manor houses:
they will ever bear my trademark clots of paint,
halts of hesitation as I read my subjects,
some so watchful, so withdrawn,
working on their algorithms, philosophic propositions,
while they stare me out or run a nervous tongue
along a lip —

aware, perhaps, of space as cold as ice
between the sitting — or the lying — form
and my reconnaissance:
between how they present and what I see:
lines of tension, tics and tones, a hooded grief,
the crease whose agitation
I can best express

/continued

by scumbling; all the while
recalling Winston's hunched aggression
briefly seen:
destroyed because it told the truth
about indwellingness;

and to this end
to seek the ens,
I prime my canvasses afresh,
daub the fat new tubes of colour on a slate,
carmine red for robes and sashes,
glaucous green and ivory,
every kind of livery, for skins:

mix the paint, as Turner did,
with spittle;
tame the sable brushes with saliva,
keep the stipppler on its toes to spread the blush
which owes as much to lust
as fire,

finely trim the pointer's hair to stab an eyelight
in an eye,
a look
that would ignite a mausoleum
let alone a studio.

Storm Warning

.... I tell them
who are standing in the field at dusk
as wind gets up
I say to them
who look at me with hostile eyes
I plead with them as thunder cracks
and rain smites down
and blanks the moon
they look at me with hollow eyes
and turn their backs
and march in line between the dunes
not breaking step
along the track
across the spit
towards the wreck
and out to sea.

pressure dropping
ocean rising
happening
now.

MARRIAGE OF TRUE MINDS

> *"Let me not to the marriage of true minds*
> *Admit impediments..."*
> *William Shakespeare: Sonnet 116*

Heading South: for Muir

As a young man,
he had heard the talk of crossing borders
south to freedom;
old,
recalls the early mornings in Madrid,
loading up his truck
with fearful children,

driving southwards through La Mancha,
wild land
where swallows whipped the palms' unruly hair
and sand-winds shook the windows'
celluloid;
children sucking oranges,
tumbling out to safety
in Valencia;

breeze of dusk across his shoulders
as he filled the tank —
no fuel in shuttered villages
no hay —

north again with harvest grain for cities under siege,
seeing through the dusty windscreen
arcs of gunfire,
sapphire blue,
raze the sky.

Kinship

We were always looking
for each other:
in our years apart
we shared the same magnetic field
though neither knew.

My parents spoke of you:
a boy of promise.
Who is he, this clever cousin?
Why should I remember that,
of all the words I ever spoke?

I became betrothed
to someone else,
wrestled with the thought:
I know I owe a prior debt of love.

Didn't find the answer
in the portrait of our forebear
even though he stared me in the face
your steady gaze,
your hands, a mouth we share.

We came together,
sorrowing —
it was written in the stars —
briefly shone together
as a constellation.

Now, although we fear the end,
we dare to hope against all odds
the shared magnetic field
may yet exert its hold.

Rhapsody

I shall not walk with bare feet in wet woods again (*)
nor feel the brushing shuffle of the leaves,
the certainty of tread
through roots of hazelnut and bracken
knotted to the thicket floor; nor

chant a lyric to the sickle-moon
which cracked its dazzling whip across the sea,
as Channel waters slapped my loins
and I imagined lust to be
a mere athletic feat.

As well that love came late
when speed and suppleness were on the wane,
and barefoot walks in rough terrain
or swimming in a darkened sea
could not be borne.

Forget the iris of Illyria, the oily myrrh —
no time to polish up the act —
revel in the ecstasy
that clinging to the mast will bring:
know that love is for the taking
as the clock strikes midnight
and the lamp is sputtering.

* *phrase from the Journal of Katherine Mansfield*

Circus

When it was over,
the acrobatic high-wire act,
we left the rumpled bed and skipped
along the promenade:
tasted the salt of the morning
the length of our tongues,

we headed back to the fairground,
walked between the awakening
caravans.

They were taking the covers off the carousel,
giving the prancing horses
a rubbing down.
Acrobats were limbering up,
turning head-over-heels,
a juggler throwing his balls in the air.

We smiled;

and in the brilliant morning sun
the lolling clown
was brushing out his mop of orange hair.

He saw us:
raised his comic eyebrows,
luscious lips still visibly drawn
on his raddled face.

What a performance,
we said.

According to Luke

Consider, if you will, the lily of the field:
how it grows in divers soils,
no need of toil, a border queen
attended on by cluster-heads,
sweetly-smelling coriander,
comfrey, lesser celandine,
the flower which lay at William's feet,
his careless prodigal.

Concupiscent, the lily grows
in every quarter of the globe: a few
prefer to seed and shine in stony places;
some, the northern ones,
incline to make their beds in leafy mould
beneath a canopy of oak and ash,
trumpets muted
by the shade.

Pick them now when they're unsure
what colour they will be:
what freckles wear around their lips;
allow them time to flaunt
their pollen tips, to spin their scent
where you can breathe it in, my Solomon,
giving thought not for the morrow,
but to how it all began

Belief

We read the book (*) together
on a close and cloudless evening
in a garden
on the outskirts of Nairobi.
Simon, the askari
in his tribal kit
is standing at the gate.

And in that fragile peace
we trudge the paths of learning,
rehearse Judeo-Christian legends —
seas rolled back as if by magic,
trumpets blasting through the walls
of Jericho —

familiar myths
to readers in the northern hemisphere,
of lesser power
in the urgent air of Africa
where scent of oleander with its toxic leaf
invades imagination,

as we try
to reconcile belief and narrative
with what is known
or what decided how and when to start
the whole thing rolling,
how continue for so long
against the odds,
the brawls, the battles,
physical and metaphysical,

the Marvellous allure
of giddy Heavens,
tinsel wings,
stern reminder of the scientific things —
miracles we do not understand.

We close the book and sleep.
Simon guards us,
spear in hand.

**Can Scientists Believe? essays edited by Sir Nevill Mott, FRS, 1991.*

Chicxulub

I was pedalling —
as in my dreams I often do —
through a dried-out river course
and up above,
passing by the moon's lopsided stare,
were mammoths,
dodos, pterodactyls,
dinosaurs and brontosauri
trundling, nose to tail,
hoofing dust.

Then came the explosion.

Oh, dear Lord, I said in my dream.
This is the end of the world,

The end of the world,
I said to you in the morning light,
the first of millennium year.

Au contraire, you said.

Go back in time and it may seem
more like the start of everything.
Sixty-four million years ago
the asteroid struck
at Chicxulub
gouging the Gulf of Mexico.

The sea rolled in,
the moon was born upon a sudden whim
and to this day
with tilted head and dialectic air
she ponders —

by the way:
there were no wheels then.

Against the Day

It's our habit —

when I leave you writing in your study,
when I post a letter, when I go to market,
smell the wheatiness of bread,
melons' ripening skin akin
to *Je Reviens;*

even when I walk the garden after rain,
sniff the silkiness of peaches
back-lit
by the post-meridian sun,
dead-head *rosa damascena,*
spare the scarlet pimpernel
to flaunt
its brazen little face at randy bees,

dust off earth-lines huddling in the vertex
of my thumb and index finger, vital
prying tool that runs in thought
along the runnel of my chin, a

sensor good for reading mood and music,
chords of intimation
from arrhythmic heart-beats: this

the brightness, only, that our state allows:
to plait a rope of sand, to write
our names on moving water —

every time we part
forfend the day.

Candlelight

They dine by candlelight:
the tallow weeps.
They eat a gamey pheasant
hung too long,
plums plucked late and musty
from the tree.

The claret has a bramble-deep maturity;
they take their glasses to the open window:
fly again to distant islands,
lie on buoyant water, feel
the old heat purling
through the skin —

the candle flickers in the wind.

Dawn

A flutter breaks the surface of our sleep.
Fear is tangible. He stoops, and with his
certain tenderness, he cups the bird —
a marten living underneath our eaves —
one hand across the breast, the other
spanning agitated wings. He frees
the wanderer, which hovers in the air,
then finds a gust and switches on to power.

A blackbird flutes a prelude and the chorus
catch the fugue from tree to tree.
Lying fesse-wise on our feather bed,
we listen to the serenade. I touch
the hand so ready to engage, to show
how love should be and how to let it go.

Garden of the Astrolabe

In the shuttered afternoon
a daddy-long-legs treads a skillet-rim,
hair-fine legs and wings
a Leonardo etching;
in the yard, a truss of green tomatoes
pines for sun;
I finger them
as later in the dusk I touch your skin,
freckled like my own
by fitful light.

Behind your eyes, you feel the flutter
of the humming bird:
count the hours in the garden of the astrolabe —
twist my golden ring.

The wind gets up; an apple drops.
The crane-fly folds its wings and drowns.
A quarter moon side-slips through the dark.

Epiphany

Bells are silent. You are sleeping.
in the never-quite-light afternoon,
I rake the compost,
bury egg-shells under brittle beech.

A blackbird watches from the apple-tree.
Glossy lordling of the heap,
he wants me gone so he can hurl the muck about,
intimidate the redwing
landing lightly
nipping scarlet berries
from the rowan tree.

Indoors, I peel some tiny tangerines,
in case you wake up
peckish,
like the birds —
stretch beside you on our feather bed.

Going Down

When we go down,
let it be hand-in-hand
to the sound of our airborne cries:
the drop will pass more affably
that way,
the landing be
a sweet concatenation.

Let the end be quick:
no lingering disease,
no ravage, wastage, rot, repulsion:
a sudden and savage event
is what we need —
no time for footling
contemplation.

Head-stall, head-on hit —
such a clincher makes you quail —
but consider, my love,
the catharsis,
the trail
we two would blaze
in that consummation.

Amanuensis: for Muir

He said:
I leave you my unfinished story:
hope that you may bring it
to completion.

Style is spare: a lawyer's habit
is to fashion clauses
as a dry-stone-waller builds his earthwork —
so

no intervention there;

but, by the end of chapter three,
our plotters have begun to show their hands,
high-up folk who meet in colonnaded
palaces,
who deal in secret over rights
to dig and bore
even as the ice-crack widens at the southern Pole:

floats a jagged island
deep enough to keep its bearings.

Guide my lovers,
on their splinter of Antarctica,
move them northward on the current
to the Tropics — be

my amanuensis —

keep them
as they circumnavigate
the Land of Fire,
Magellan's beacon sighted from the sea:
and in the warm air of the Gulf of Panama
succumb,
their ice-bed melt
to form a new Pacific stream.

When they come together
let there be
a clash of symbols echoing
through depth-cold sea.

You will know
how to write that passage.

Blueprint

He makes a sketch of how he wants the room to be:
the painting of a Polish plain
with mop-head trees of peacock-blue —
improbable but true as he can testify —

a pair of Famille Rose which, like tattoos
inscribed in gentle greens and pinks and blues
upon their bellies, picture day-to-day activities:
sewing, reading, waiting
on the lord and master:

looks on these familiar indoor things
as not so long ago he climbed the garden steps
and from his sturdy bench beneath the damson tree
would smell the trampled camomile,
watch the willows sail;

asks: *how will it be?*
writes across the paper: *not to scale.*

AFTERMATH

"For thy sweet love remember'd such wealth brings
That then I scorn to change my state with kings".
William Shakespeare: Sonnet 29

21 October 2008

I am lying on my back as you did when you died —
I may not twist my hip
until the new ball settles in —
that is how your hand held mine,
square-tipped fingers covering my narrower fist
as we would walk together, nightly,
in Elysium.

Iambs, cantos, Alexandrine rhythms,
scampered through our minds as we talked far
into the early hours,
reborn, in your case, come morning,
never to recur, in mine.

That night, I held your hand as it grew cold,
our finger arcs reversed.
I hope you knew,
at the moment of your little sigh,
that I had tried
to follow you.

Little Tree

I do not know its name.
Its leaves are trefoil-shaped
and spread their hands
as if to make a plea;
the flowers are stars
which open in the light,
tremble at the rumble
of the traffic,
droop at dusk.

Their movement comforts me
on Saturday, a static day,
when I am still and grieving
still the while
the uncomplaining tree
shrivels in the wind and rain
because it may not cry.

Amulet

After the nightmare
check the every-day:
the jumper, socks and
toothbrush, shoes
with rubber soles;
eat a freshly-heated croissant,
take a breath of air —
hey —
the day is dull,
a little drizzle,
usual for a Saturday
before the clocks go on.

Rummage in the drawer,
find the ancient Omega —
dimming face
and smudgy Roman numerals —
make sure I wear it
on my arm
before I sleep again.

Getting There

The chaste die in their sleep,
if they're lucky,
deeply uncomplaining
of the years of wakefulness,
of tripping on uncertainty,
measuring the distance
up and down the step,
bridging gaps between the said
and the withheld,
observing
how the fingers of the left
and of the right
are differently wired;
how the magpie in the winter garden
sways on top of Flora,
little statue,
pisses on her neat coiffure
for want of anything more lewd;
seeing, sightless,
if they're lucky
small volcanic sunsets form
and sputter.

About Half-Past Four

Think of it as syncopation, an
arpeggio up and down the spine.
All you have to do is cease to listen:

fade sensation into silence,
like the composition Four Point Thirty-Three
in which your violinists,

clarinettists sit, as Cage decreed,
for precisely that duration,
hands and lips relaxed, making only

tiny unintended sounds: pops and flicks
and grace notes in a minor key.
What happens in that space and what you hear

is up to you: in place of pain,
your lover's voice, perhaps, the little sigh
as he was dying:

and remember that it's half-past four,
or thereabouts, a time when what you hear
is muted by the dawn, but what you know

is cruelly exact. Four point thirty-three,
the time allowed, no less, no more,
for inward agony.

Afterthought

seeing you
squatting on the stairs between the fourth and second riser,
feet apart,
resting from the small domestic jobs of Saturday:

bottles brought up from the cellar
polished flutes
explosive corks;

mindful of the spark of pleasure kept alight
which carries sense from one four-liner
to another.
Satinwood, you called our years together,
deeply bloomed with love.

hearing still
strains and rhapsodies,
exultant cries,
within, within,
disputations at Scutari — *je suis avocat anglais* —
sound waves
that will never wholly die away,

habitual as heart-beats
and as quickening.

Endogen

I touched the sound of joy one morning
as I woke:
heard the perfect pitch
of plainsong's mid-
line pause,
intake of breath;

I touched the sound of joy this morning too:
fluting from a hollow stem,
a sip of clarinet,
the oboe's cry of love, its embouchure:
new wood ravishing
the lip.

FIGMENTS

> *"Figment: Something moulded or fashioned eg. An image 1664; a product of invention, a fiction, ME" OED*

Green Apple (Oil on board 5" x 7", Fred Dubery)

The artist lays his gingham cloth of viridescent green
across the line between the known and the withheld:
strokes a slight undoing
where the checks behind a drinking glass
refract and blur —
a whirlpool of a platter
disappearing;

at the golden mean
a Venus apple spills a purple shadow,
striæ brushed across its belly,
yellow shoulder faintly lit by eau-de-nil green,
inviting greedy hands and mouths:
a libertine.

Madness at Night

A lustful moon licks up the sea,
the Bore is bowling up the Severn

Old one dreams of running,
curling, curving, vaulting

niello-bellied clouds release their rain,
the scent from camomile,

getting wind of treasures found in hidden places
resolutions at the heart of things

water-meadows fill and glisten;
dawn comes up the colour of calendula.

brindle cat with grape-green eyes
pounces on her prey

lies recumbent by the stove,
twitches in her dream of stalking.

Rebel Sun

The jigsaw
won't accommodate the maverick;
the dingy flat-bits, locking neatly,
grumble at the cuboid one
who puts on airs,
a Miró habit,
sees himself as Red Sun, robed
in bold vermilion,

Shocking,
say the interlockers,
far too bright, not one of us:
can't allow this garish cube,
this soi-disant surrealist,
to overshadow us,
prevent us from achieving
our integrity.

The maverick,
expelled from mannerism,
insufflates his wicked — and it must be said,
misshapen — red balloon,
blazes, meteoric,
into space,
towards a new dimension
of his own;

/continued

negotiates his roster
with the Golden Sun.
She does daylight:
always has and always will,
Moon's a parish lantern on a starry night,
immoveable.

His role,
as the day spins into night
and night reclaims the day,
to stipple rosy-fingered dawn,
to daub the dusk
as poets write by fading light
and birds are hushed
in awe;

to shine with guilty pleasure
on the hexagon he left
below.

In the Scanner

Won't look up,
never by a lash's flicker —

go to your cathedral,
calm crusader,
lie upon your table tomb,
your whippet at your feet:
there is hallowed space above —

below
the atmosphere
within the metal coffin
palls —

steel yourself to touch the vaulting,
feel how tender
years of rising candle-smoke
have made it —
listen —

hear the growling
of the haruspex

the plainsong of the choir —
from side to side
voices answer one another,
trebles, altos,
point and counterpoint
descant

descend:
locusts patten on the bones,
extort
the secrets of the skeleton —

/continued

beyond the city, way out on the plain,
alien hands have drawn
surreal patterns in the body
of the corn.

I fear
the seer may find the gap
between the walnut
and the skull
where shameful fungi
lie:

foreshadow death —
at last
the sweet intake of breath.

Weaving

Weave the green and sinuous withies
split from cloudy Langport levels
fit to bear a plaited bloomer,
hollow head of yellow pumpkin,
candles shining through the smile,
celebrating Hallowe'en;

overlap the strands of raffia,
stripped from palm trees by the ocean:
flaunt voluptuous mango, pawpaw,
ugli fruit and pomegranate,
on the high road to Nyeri,
steeply falling to the Rift;

tautly weave the mournful sackcloth
cut from Ganges delta hemp-lands:
carriers for herbal potions,
cures for dhobi itch and palsy,
dumdum fever, sleeping sickness,
broken hearts and frail minds;

scythe the reed-stalks smelling sweetly
on the tilth of Salthouse marshes;
dredge the wetlands where the curlews,
needle-leggéd, brake their landings,
skid on water, agitated
by the gun-fire closing in.

Master Builder

I walk about, I leave my imprint
on the jamb of every door,
close the shutters perfectly designed
never to knock
the slender glazing-bars:
prepare to leave.

Master Builder,
do you admire
the painting of the great saloon in Adam-green,
the restoration of the ceiling rose,
the felling of the sycamore
that undermined the footings
of your house?

In its stead,
I planted sweetly-smelling small-leaf lime.
You will know this tree:
specie *T. Cordata:*
Grinling Gibbons' leaves and flowers,
his viols and curlicues
inspired your plainer joinery.

I have left
in its propriety
the curving baluster;
the doors askew within their architraves;
the cornicing;
the flagstones in the cellar
with their reek of earth;

the fanlight holds
the flawed prismatic glass you fitted
when you built this house
two hundred years and more ago:
you know
it throws a pattern on your marble floor
of fantail doves in flight —
nothing that you touched
was unintended.

Pavlopetri - city under the sea

Divers, fin-feet, scan the underwater streets,
fingers stalk the sea-bed,
scoop up Bronze-age loom-weights
shaped like doughnuts,
beam the city's achromatic symmetry
of courts and quads;

speculate by virtual means
on structures and their uses:
houses, markets, treasuries;
happen on a scribble in the mud —
shout distortedly to one another through their masks —
it's a giant O
mouthpiece of a monumental vessel
buried up to shoulder-height
that none would dare to touch with hands or tools;
and so

a monster water-dredger
sucks and blows until the pithos sheds its robe,
emerges naked from the ash,
voluptuous in shoulder-shards
and sliver-hips.

Not so the dead whose sober bones
lie seriatim in their rock-cut tombs,
parted from those infants born to mortify
beyond
the angle of forensic light,
beyond the shadow of a shade,
a grave
where playful micro-organisms bloop,

make a motley of their patch of water,
take
one more step towards
unmaking.

Under the Thorn Tree: the founding of Nairobi Hospice

The women gathered underneath the tree:
it wove its knuckled skein of bark
upwards to the canopy —
to some from northern lands
it smelt of lavender;
others felt the eucalyptus sparkle in the air,
so windless in the Masai Mara
at Epiphany.

Muslin-wrapped against the heat,
the women talked of pain that should not be endured;
and then,
in ones and twos, sought out the city men
who made decisions

while the women waded, knee deep,
through the trickle-lanes
of orange river-mud
in shanty-towns. The clay,
they said, is soft enough for burial —
but living souls should lie
on fleecy pallets,
cool and dry.

They heard a drum-beat from the bush,
a trumpeting from underneath the tree
as hot as still as on the first Epiphany.

Discarded Shoes

Prostitutes in Majengo, Kenya, who possess a natural immunity to AIDS/HIV, co-operate with a research programme.

Ola will not wear the shoes
of those who had the virus
better sell the sneakers clogs

and sandals worn at sole and heel
to passing strangers on the highway —
one way of surviving

though the other way will buy
more posho for the kids
her own and those whose mothers

left their shoes behind
and in the darkness of the shack
Ola dreams about a time

when all will be immune and she will live
beside a lake of pink flamingos
in the valley of the Rift

and though she cannot count the men
who've weighed her down
she freely gives her blood

marvelling at cells so carefree so impervious —
but as ever walking barefoot
never shod.

Figments

I do figments: I transfigure tubas, trumpets,
flugelhorns and mandolins, strangle
the triumphant sounds their makers gave them;
create new significance; hang them on the walls
of long-abandoned storage places by the river
where the glass is broken and the litter blows;

make my mark by scratching walls as lifers do,
painfully with thumb and finger, crossing off
the years of retribution with a wrinkled hand:
scatter planks, rife with splinters, make a scimitar,
an arrowhead, a hexagon, a theorem: *quod*
erat demonstrandum as the saying goes.

My lover left three tanzanites, pips of purest
azure blue with faces scrupulously cut
to warm the sun. Unalterable, they sit on top
of little props of silver-gold, smiling
at the light they seek to catch. I turn my hand
this way and that. I watch them glow.

METAMORPHOSIS

Metamorphosis

Through sculptured feet the fusilier
feels the rush of little rivers
pulsing more insistently
as surface clash and clangour die away
and plane-trees shiver in the after-quiet of dusk
in early spring.

He scrapes the skerry from his boots and jumps;
lands on paving stones
a chequerboard
that other feet had cracked and pitted over time
while his had been embedded in the plinth;

suffers shock of river-wind
as limestone softens into skin and bone —
even eyebrows work their magic
independently,
signal to a girl with damson skin,
a brimming girl with crooked smile and whitened palms,
crease-marks inked across the fingers
taking hold of his.

He summons up the trick of swivelling his shoulders,
bending knees and flexing feet,
walking to her rhythmic stride across the bridge —
spring tide whipping up the dark green river,
steamers flying faster than he's ever seen.

/continued

Walking hand in hand
in dank, neglected tongues of land,
they forage fruit three-quarters sound,
bullace, cloudberry, dewberry, buds of hawkbit,
ear of Judas listening on an elder-tree,

shun the white destroying angel,
breathe
the honey-smell of lady's bedstraw,

blow the ashes till the sparks fly up:
she
so wild in love, agile as an acrobat,
he
intent on searching out the pleasure
in whatever crevice it may lie,

sleeping, spent,
on paving stones
as comfortably as on a feather bed.

But there begin
in her no less than him
a gradual loss of ease,
a stiffness moving down from shoulder-yoke
to numbing funny-bone —
finger-tips that will no longer read the other's skin,
the sleep of drying eyes
that weep
though having no more tears to run.

And in the once familiar square
where charioteers still ride the sky,
she scratches out the legend of *The Unknown Fusilier,*
writes instead
Metamorphosis;
climbs the plinth,
helps him up to kneel there.

They harden into bronze, her natural element.
She lies across his thigh,
her hair a canopy, conforming limbs
their monument.

REFERENCE

Gillian Petrie – Biography

Gillian's earlier years were spent raising four children and then working in the field of cancer care. For thirty years, she worked in the hospice movement: as head of Marie Curie's national home nursing service; as a founder-trustee of Nairobi Hospice, Kenya and as founder-director of Polish Hospices Fund which organised training for Polish doctors. She and her husband, Professor Muir Hunter QC (who brought his legal expertise to the projects), were decorated by the Polish Government.

Turning to poetry in the nineties, Gillian joined Kick Start Poets of Salisbury, becoming chair in 2000-2002. During those years, the group invited many distinguished poets, among others: John Freeman, Alan Brownjohn. Matthew Sweeney, Alice Oswald, UA Fanthorpe, Lawrence Sail etc. She was subsequently taught by Professor Sir Andrew Motion (then Poet Laureate) and Professor Jo Shapcott on the MA creative writing course at Royal Holloway, University of London. Gillian is grateful for these poets' excellent tutelage and for the help and friendship of her fellow students. She undertook a further course with Jo Shapcott and Daljit Nagra at Faber & Faber.

Gillian's work has been published in anthologies: *Bedford Square 2* edited by Sir Andrew Motion (John Murray, 2007), *A Luminous Man - Muir Hunter, recalled with love* (Palewell Press, 2013) and in *Starters,* the publications of Kick Start Poets of Salisbury from 1998 onwards.

This first collection comes to press with the support and encouragement of Camilla Reeve, editor, Palewell Press, to whom so many thanks.

Palewell Press

Palewell Press is an independent publisher handling poetry, fiction and non-fiction with a focus on human rights, social history and the environment. The Editor may be reached at enquiries@palewellpress.co.uk

www.ingramcontent.com/pod-product-compliance
Ingram Content Group UK Ltd.
Pitfield, Milton Keynes, MK11 3LW, UK
UKHW020238250726
13967UKWH00001B/446

9 781911 587019